the Eternal Flower

the Eternal Flower

Koji Arai

Photography Kiyokazu Nakajima

stichting kunstboek

Foreword はじめに

I was born in the Japanese city of Kōbe in 1960. In those days, foreigners were still rarely seen in most Japanese cities, but Kōbe was an exception - an exotic, cosmopolitan port where passers-by were often from all corners of the world.

It was only natural, I think, that as I grew up, I found myself fascinated by far away lands, to the point where I realized that I wished for more than travel, I wanted to live abroad.

My first dream was to go to the United States, but that had to be abandoned when my applications were unsuccessful. Then a mentor whom I met in Tokyo told me that Brazil offered residency rights after one year's work at a flower grower. After training in Japan for a year, I set out for Sao Paulo.

In Sao Paulo, I worked for a farmer who specialized in potted flowers, a colonia whose family had immigrated from Japan. As we communicated in Japanese, my language skills did not improve, and I began to wonder what had been the point of coming to Brazil. My employer was concerned about me, and suggested that I work at a florist in the city, and offered to arrange a job with a friend of his. I leapt at the chance, because I wanted to speak Portuguese, and it would also be a way to earn a living. I am now obsessed with plants, and the possibilities of floral design, but this is how it all began.

When I started out, I could not even tell roses and tulips apart, let alone make a bouquet. The shop did not spoon feed me instructions regarding what I had to do, so I learnt by stealing glances at what my colleagues were doing, and how they accomplished their tasks. This experience, I believe, established my stance regarding work.

After returning to Japan, I joined Daiichi Engei, working on decorations for weddings and other events at luxury hotels, as well as product development. 28 years have gone by. I currently head the Design Team, and my responsibilities include event decorations, floral design demonstrations, teaching at schools, and design/planning of products.

In a certain sense, this collection stands apart from my body of work as a flower designer. In this book, I wish to share my personal and innermost thoughts, emotions, and wishes, channeled through my desire to express myself through flowers and plants. The beauty of their colours, which at times borders on the grotesque, their enthrallingly eccentric forms, their life, their death, the tales that emerge from our interaction – this is what I have tried to give shape and a voice.

If these works help to disclose the fascinating aspects of flowers and plants that we often remain unaware of, and if, perhaps, my hands can serve to bring together the fragility of life, and its far too fleeting beauty in a manner that will help to form 'eternal memories', it would be more than I ever dared to dream of.

Koji Arai

私は1960年、日本の神戸という町に生まれました。今のように街で外国の人を見かけることはあまりない時代でしたが、その当時から神戸は、外国人が行き交う異国情緒あふれる港町でした。

このような環境で幼少期を過ごしたため、自然と海外への興味が湧き、いつしか旅行ではなく、海外に住んでみたいと思うようになりました。

はじめはアメリカで夢を実現しようと試みましたが、移住権が取得できずに断念。そんな時、東京で知り合った恩師から、ブラジルであれば、一年、花の農家で研修すれば移住権が得られると教えてもらいました。日本で一年の研修の後、サンパウロに渡航しました。

サンパウロでは、日系コロニアの花鉢の生産農家で働きました。日本語で仕事ができたため、現地の言葉を覚えず、何のためにブラジルまで来たのだろうと思い悩むようになりました。すると、そんな私を心配した雇い主がある時、「街の花屋で働いてみては？」と知り合いのお店を紹介してくれました。ポルトガル語を話したいと思っていた私は、生活の糧になるということもあり、お願いすることに。今でこそ植物の魅力にとりつかれ、フラワーデザインの道中にいる私ですが、はじめの一歩はこんな風にスタートしたのでした。

花屋で働きはじめた頃の私は、バラとチューリップの見分けもつかない、花束ひとつ作れない状態でした。しかし、仕事を手取り足取り丁寧に教えてくれるわけではないので、周りの人のやり方を目で盗んで覚えたものです。その経験から、仕事を学ぶ姿勢が身につきました。

帰国後に入社した第一園芸では、ラグジュアリーホテルの結婚式をはじめとした空間装飾や商品開発などに携わり、28年が経ちました。現在はデザイン室長としてイベントの装飾、フラワーデザインのデモンストレーション、スクールの講師、商品の企画デザインなどさまざまな業務を担当しています。

本書では、職業としてのフラワーデザイナーという立場から離れ、自分の心に湧き上がってくる想いや表現したいという欲求を作品に投影しました。美しくも不気味な色や珍妙な形、花の生死、私と花の間で生まれるストーリー、それらをこの一冊の中に表現しています。

本書をご覧になってくださる皆さまに、植物にひそんでいる魅力を発見し感じていただけたら、そして、儚い命、一瞬の美しさをこの手によって「永遠の記憶」へ導くことができたらなら、この上ない幸せです。

新井光史

Chapter 1

Colour 色

Colours are a constant inspiration. They spur me to create and express. The world around us is overflowing with glorious colours, but I remain particularly drawn and attached to the palette of nature. Plants are nature's creations, perfect in their very existence and every single colour pulsing with life.

Sometimes, I focus on a single colour, sometimes; I let a variety of tones interact with another set of tones. The purpose of any of my interventions, I think, is to draw attention to the hidden or overlooked aspects of plants.

花の色はいつも、表現への意欲を掻き立ててくれる。
こんなにも世界は色であふれているのに、
私はとりわけ自然が創り出した色に、いつも心惹かれる。
自然が創造した植物は、存在そのものが完成品であり、
一つひとつの色に命が宿っている。
時にひとつの色を際立たせ、時にさまざまな色を出合わせる。
私が手を加える意味とは、
植物の秘めたる魅力を引き出すことだと思う。

State of Mind

心地

Sonorous Timbres

鋳声

Nocturnal Blue

青夜

Pristine

清廉

Helios

日輪

Caprice

移気

Luxuriant Beauties

艶色

L'Heure Exquise

黄昏

The Connoisseur

粋人

Lifeforce

生彩

The Graces

風雅

Full Fathom Five

海底

Chapter 2

Time 時間

My work is only possible by sacrificing the lives of flowers. Itadaki-masu ('I humbly receive') is a phrase that the Japanese speak before a meal, expressing their gratefulness towards what they are about to eat. In the same sprit, I also say a silent itadaki-masu to the flowers to thank them for offering their lives.
Expressing time passing by teaches us that life and death are always intertwined. Even after the flowers decay and disappear, their beauty remains alive in our hearts and minds.

私の仕事は、花の命をいただくことで成り立っている。
だから、日本人が「素材の命を頂戴する」という意味で
食事の前に発する言葉「いただきます」の精神と同じく、
花の命に対して、「いただきます」と心でつぶやく。
時の経過を表現することは、
生と死が、いつでも隣り合わせにあることを教えてくれる。
果ては朽ちて、存在を失っても、
花の美しさは心のなかに生き続ける。

Innocence

無垢

Lifespan

生涯

Pollen

花粉

Sweets to the Sweet

甘美

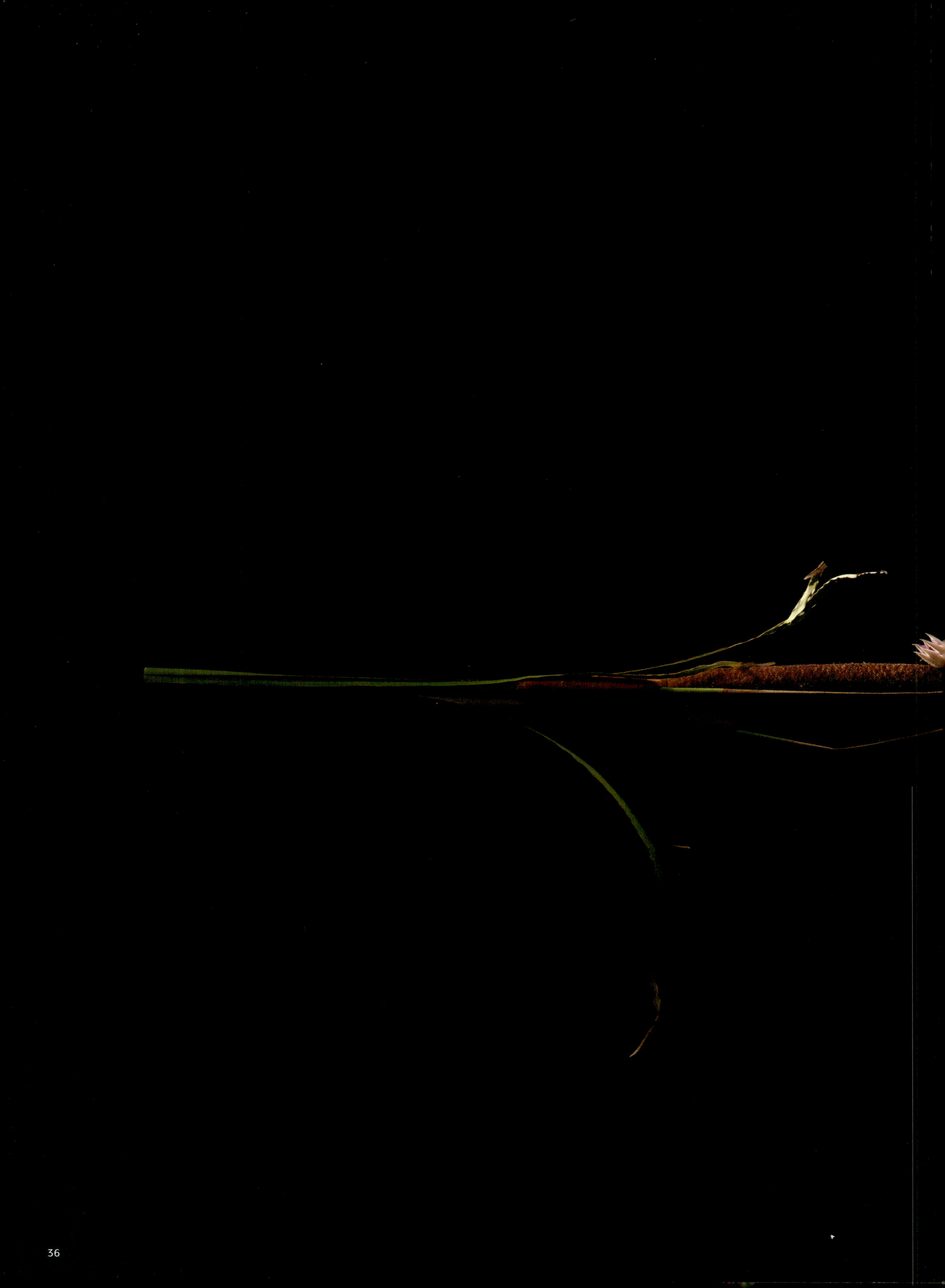

Moment of Truth

刹那

Precocity

早熟

Lusciousness

爛熟

Nostalgia

追憶

Elysian Fields

黄昏

Cycle of Life

輪廻

Chapter 3

Form 形

Plants exist in their current form thanks to eons of evolution in order to survive.

Unlike animals, plants cannot move. Their survival is made possible by desperately reaching out through roots, stems, branches and leaves. They may result from nothing more than a natural selection process, but their shapes and forms are important factors in defining the individuality of plants, and, I believe, an important part of my attraction to them.

I introduce plants to one another, group them together, and continue to explore their fascinating forms and possibilities.

長い進化の歴史の中で、植物が生き延びるために選んできた姿。
植物は動物のようには動けない代わりに、
根や茎や枝葉を伸ばして、懸命に生きる道を探してきた。
植物にとって当然の成り行きだとしても、
その姿形は個性を決める重要な因子であり、
そこに魅力がつまっているように感じる。
私は植物を出合わせ、群れを作り、
造形としてのおもしろさを模索している。

Swan Maiden

羽衣

Shadowlands

幽玄

Celestial Chimes

美音

Gallantry

凛然

Assimilation

同化

The Ark

箱舟

Coup de Foudre

電撃

Falling Autumn

秋雫

Antennae

触手

Otherworldly Mysteries

影像

Chapter 4

Tales 物語

Throughout history, flowers have embodied our wishes and desires. When we work together, there are moments that I can hear them speak.
Flowers are supposed to lack voices, but there are times when they chatter away, and times when they prefer to be monosyllabic.
In this chapter there are some tales that are born from encounters between plants and from the conversations that I have with them. No story can ever be the same.
These works are crystallizations of my thoughts and emotions.

花は昔から、人の想いや願いを込められてきた存在だ。
花と向き合っていると、その声が聞こえることがある。
物言わぬはずの花たちが、時に饒舌に、
時にぽつりぽつりと私に語りかけてくる。
植物同士が出合い、
そして私と植物が対話することで紡がれる物語。
同じストーリーは二度と生まれない。
その一瞬いっしゅんの想いを作品に託して。

Confrontation

对峙

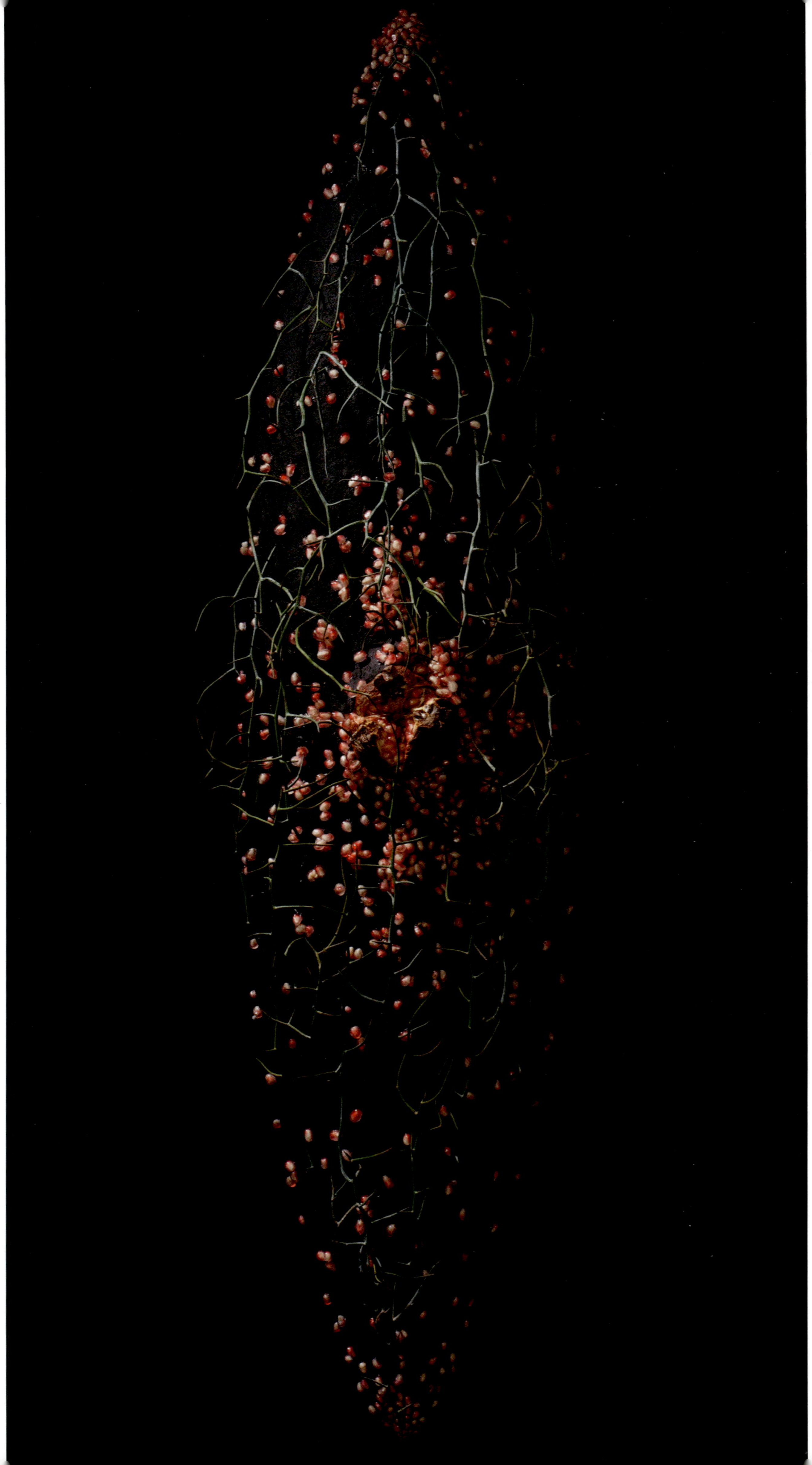

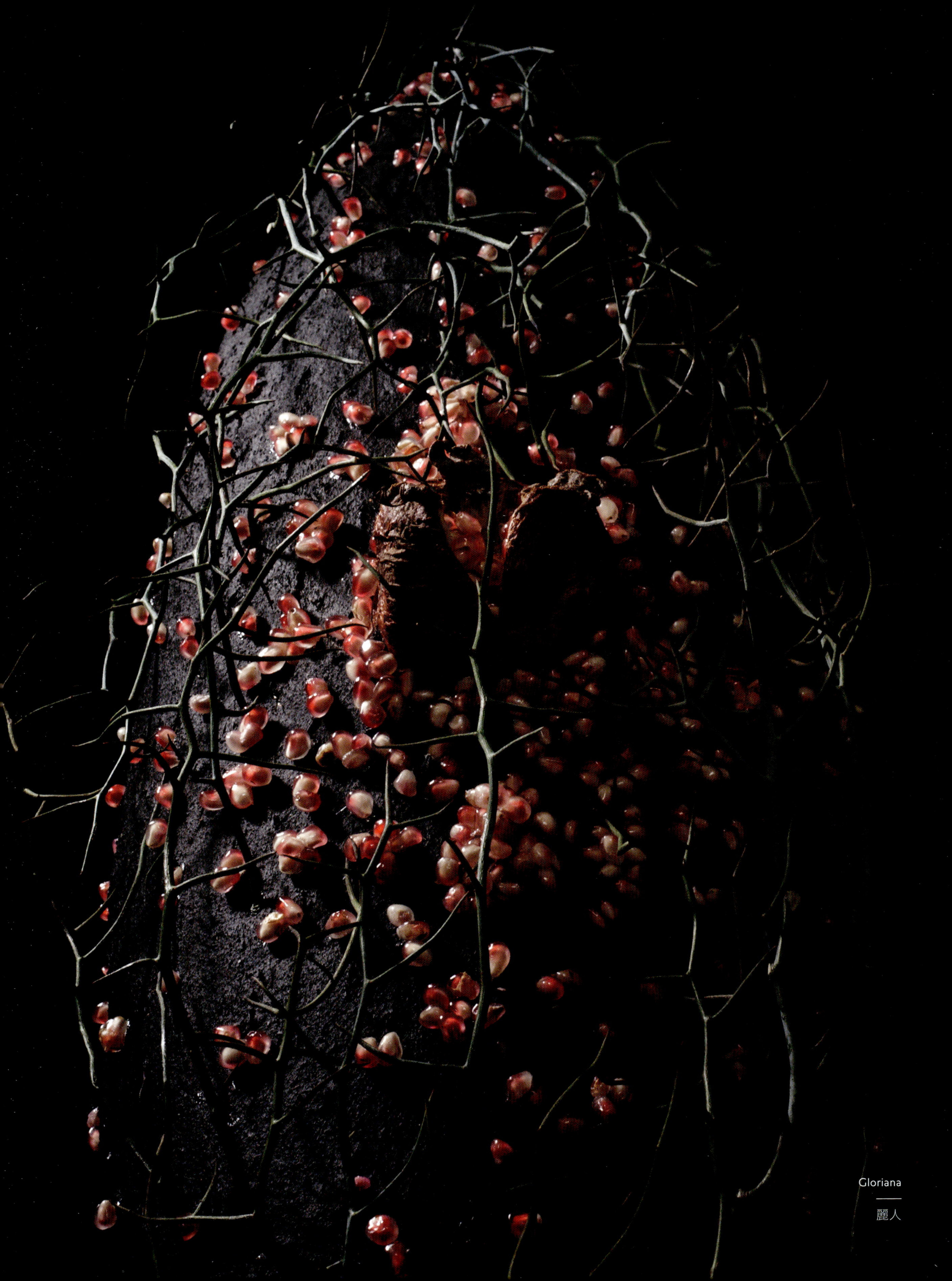

Gloriana

麗人

Fallen Glory

盛衰

Rhythmic Moves

律動

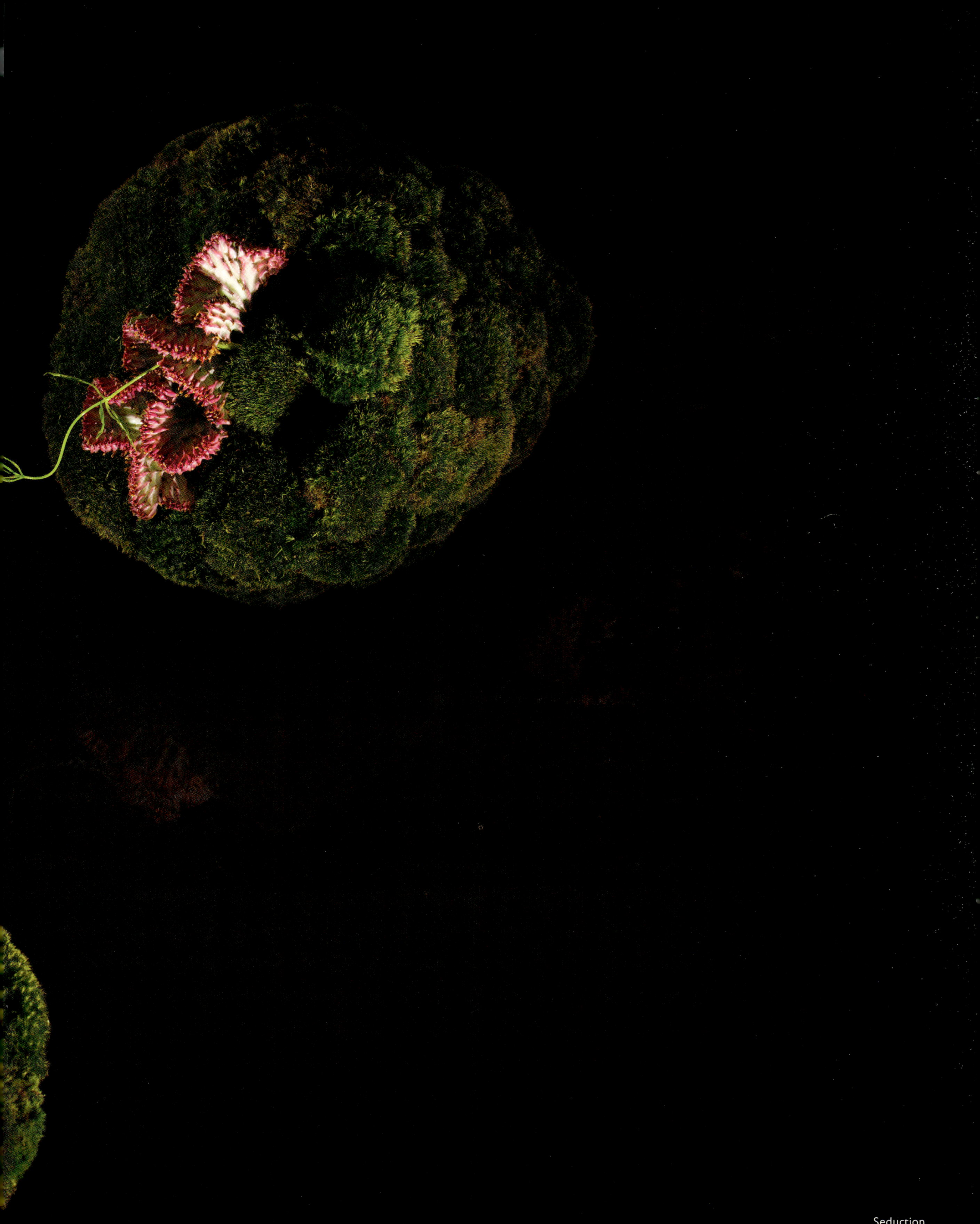

Seduction

誘惑

Equilibrium

均衡

The Butterfly Dream

儚世

The Encounter

遭遇

Intersection

交叉

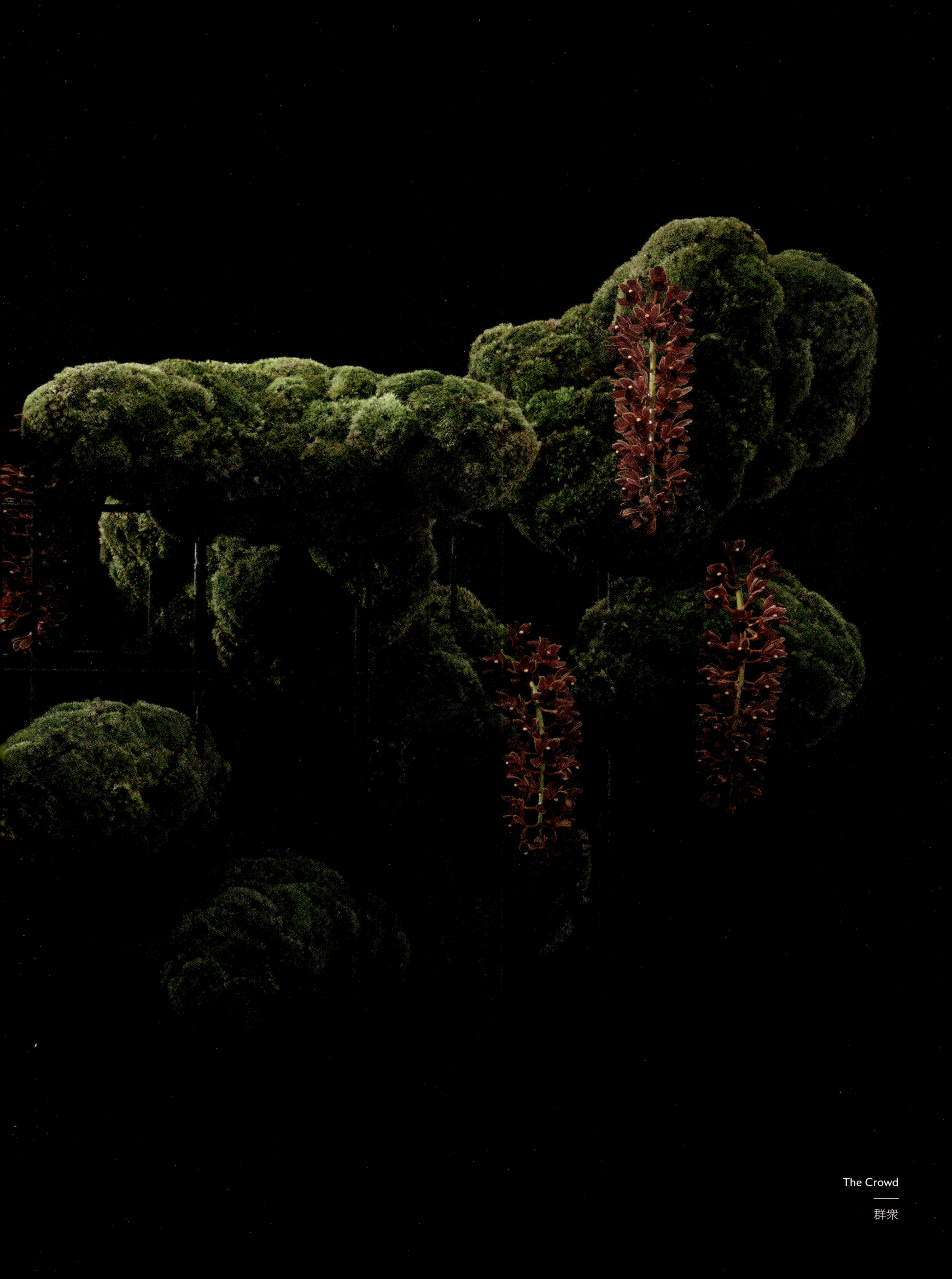

The Crowd

群衆

Silences

沈黙

Flowers

p.7
State of Mind | 心地
Astrantia / Fritillaria / Hedera helix (berries) / Helleborus niger / Paphiopedilum / Scabiosa / Tradescantia / Vanda / Viola tricolor

p.8-9
Sonorous Timbres | 錆声
Malus (crab apple) / Rosa / Scabiosa / Skimmia / Smilax china / spray roses / Viburnum tinus (berries) / Viola tricolor

p.10-11
Nocturnal Blue | 青夜
Allium (Snake Ball) / Anemone / Aquilegia / Centaurea cyanus / Cerinthe / Eryngium maritimum / Hyacinthus / Hydrangea / Iris / Jacobaea maritime (Dusty Miller) / Paphiopedilum / Scilla / Tillandsia tectorum / Vanda / Viola tricolor / Xerographica

p.12
Pristine | 清廉
Clematis / Helleborus

p.13
Helios | 日輪
Borago officinalis / Citrus medica var. sarcodactylis / Hedera helix / Hyacinthus / Justicia brandegeeana (shrimp plant) / Narcissus / Paeonia (Japanese peony) / Ranunculus / Scabiosa / Yumehotaru / Thlaspi 'Green Bell' / Tulipa / Viburnum tinus (Snowball)

p.14-15
Caprice | 移気
Ageratina altissima / Astilbe / Astrantia / Callicarpa japonica (Japanese beautyberry) / Celosia cristata / Cosmos atrosanguineus / Hydrangea (vintage) / Hypericum / Iris domestica / Japanese rose / Malus (crab apple) / Patrinia scabiosifolia (Eastern valerian) / Pennisetum glaucum (pearl millet) / rose hip / Trichosanthes pilosa (Japanese snake gourd) / Tricyrtis 'Empress' (Japanese toad lily) / Viburnum dilatatum / Viburnum opulus 'Compactum' / wild climbing rose / Xerophyllum tenax

p.16-17
Luxuriant Beauties | 艶色
Camellia / Dianthus 'Green Truffle' / Pieris japonica / Skimmia / Viburnum tinus

p.18-19
L'Heure Exquise | 黄昏
L'Heure Exquise Astilbe / Campanula trachelium (Throatwort) / Celosia cristata / Cissus rhombifolia / Cotinus / Elymus repens (Witch grass) / Equisetum / Fritillaria / Iris ochroleuca / Iris x hollandica / Justicia brandegeeana / Nigella / Scabiosa

p.20-21
The Connoisseur | 粋人
Begonia / Cattleya / Cymbidium / Epidendrum / Lachenalia aloides (Cape cows lip) / Paphiopedilum / Phalaenopsis / Prosartes (Fairybells) / Rhipsalis (Mediterranean) / Vanda

p.22-23
Lifeforce | 生彩
Ageratum / Clematis / Epidendrum / Iris / Iris germanica / Leucocoryne / Oregano 'Gymnaster' / Paeonia lactifloria / Pulsatilla vulgaris / Scabiosa / Silene armeria / Smilax china / Spirodela polyrhiza / Thlaspi 'Green Bell' / Viola

p.24-25
The Graces | 風雅
Anemone hupihensis / Astilbe / Avena (wild oats) / Callicarpa japonica / Caryopteris x clandonensis / Celosia cristata / Clematis integrifolia / Dianthus (spray carnation) / Hibiscus sabdariffa (roselle) / Hypericum / Lablab purpureus / Patrina scabiosifolia / Rosa (rose hips) / Symphoricarpos / Trichosanthes pilosa / Viburnum dilatatum

p.26-27
Full Fathom Five | 海底
Begonia / Cerinthe, Helleborus / Strelitzia / Vanda

p.29
Innocence | 無垢
Magnolia kobus

p.30-31
Lifespan | 生涯
Crataegus / Malus (crab apples) / Smilax china

p32-33
Pollen | 花粉
Lilium 'Casablanca' (flower and pollen)

p.34-35
Sweets to the Sweet | 甘美
Helianthus annuus

p.36-37
Moment of Truth | 刹那
Clematis / Typha

p.38-39
Precocity | 早熟
Momordica charantia / Smilax

p.40-41
Lusciousness | 爛熟
Anthurium / Smilax

p.42-43
Nostalgia | 追憶
Rosa /
Fragrant orange-colored
olive leafs

p.44-45
Elysian Fields | 黄昏
Chrysanthemum /
Helianthus annuus

p.46-47
Cycle of Life | 輪廻
Ampelopsis brevipedunculata

p.49
Swan Maiden | 羽衣
Spathiphyllum

p.50-51
Cultivation | 培養
Pandanus / Rubus

p.52-53
Shadowlands | 幽玄
Allium (Snake Ball) /
Scirpus tabernaemontani

p.54-55
Celestial Chimes | 美音
Brugmansia /
Saururus cernuus

p.56
Gallantry | 凛然
Ravenala madagascariensis /
Strelitzia

p.57
Assimilation | 同化
Pinus (pine needles) / gourd

p.58-59
The Ark | 箱舟
Zantedeschia

p.60-61
Coup de Foudre | 電撃
Brassia (spider orchid) /
Hedera helix (berries) /
Prunus (plum) /
Tillandsia xerographica

p.62-63
Quickening | 蠢動
Papaver (poppy)

p.64-65
Falling Autumn | 秋雫
Callicarpa japonica /
Castanea (chestnut) /
Dendrochilum / Eupatorium /
Hydrangea / Hypericum /
Paederia foetida / Setaria
italica / Tricyrtis / Typha

p.66-67
Antennae | 触手
Hordeum jubatum /
Magnolia kobus /
Viburnum dilatatum

p.68-69
Otherworldly Mysteries | 影像
Lotus seeds /
Viburnum opulus

p.71
Confrontation | 対峙
Citrus japonica /
Citrus medica var. sarcodactylis /
Gloriosa / moss

p.72-73
Gloriana | 麗人
Acacia aphylla /
Punica granatum

p.74-75
Fallen Glory | 盛衰
Cotinus / Helianthus annuus

p.76-77
Rhythmic Moves | 律動
Paphiopedilum /
Pulsatilla cernua /
Tulipa (seed)

p.78-79
Seduction | 誘惑
Euphorbia lactea / moss /
Trichocereus bridgesii
forma mostruosa

p.80-81
Equilibrium | 均衡
Actinotus helianthi /
Gossypium (cotton plant)

p.82-83
The Butterfly Dream | 儚世
Prunus (cherry blossom)

p.84-85
The Encounter | 遭遇
Pinus

p.86-87
Intersection | 交叉
Allium (Snake ball) /
Anthurium /
Argyreia nervosa /
Equisetum / Lotus /
Physocarpus opulifolius
'Diabolo' / Rubus fruticosus

p.88-89
The Crowd | 群衆
Cymbidium Dorothy
Stockstill 'Forgotten Fruit' /
moss

p.90-91
Silences | 沈黙
Argyreira nervosa /
Begonia venosa /
Cucurbita (squash)

Conclusion and Acknowledgements

Serendipity and coincidence led me to the world of flower design, but as I look back, I realize that nature has been a part my life from the very beginning.

My oldest memory that has to do with plants is having a mugwort leaf crushed and applied to a cut. The smell of freshly cut grass still takes me back to that moment. I spent my days from dawn till dusk clambering around hillsides, playing Tarzan, creating secret hideaways, catching crayfish and capturing insects. I now realize that those days of exploring and luxuriating in the wild were priceless. I also taught myself how to find materials that nature provided, and to put them to good use while having a magnificent time.

I also remember that my mother made flowers a part of life. Wild flowers in vases were part of everyday life. We also went sketching in nature together, and all the drawing and painting that I did then has, I think, been a definite influence on my work as a flower designer.

I thank fate for leading me to this profession where I can bring colour and joy to people's lives with my flowers.

Lastly, there are no words to express my gratitude towards Dai-ichi Engei for their overwhelming support during the preparation of this book. I am also heavily indebted to the great photographer Kiyokazu Nakajima for his patience and his incredible images. Special thanks also to editor Mikako Yamaguchi for her painstaking work, the translator Kayoko Yokota, and the many, many people who made this publication possible. My particular thanks go to Hiroyuki Oka, Manabu Hashiguchi, Chiyo Yoshikai and Erika Sugiyama.

Koji Arai

おわりに

偶然が重なって、フラワーデザインの世界に入りましたが、記憶の糸をたどると、私の原風景には自然がありました。

人生で一番古い植物の記憶は、傷口にヨモギの葉をすり込んでもらったこと。今でも、草刈りをしたあとの緑っぽい香りを嗅ぐと、あの頃にタイムスリップしたかのように感じます。日が暮れるまで野山を駆けまわり、ターザンごっこ、秘密基地作り、ザリガニ釣り、昆虫採集に夢中になっていました。自然の中にどっぷりとつかった貴重な時間。自然にある素材を使って、工夫しながら楽しむということを学びました。

次に思い出される植物の記憶は、母が暮らしの中に花を取り入れてくれていたことです。野原に咲いている花をさりげなく花瓶に飾っていたことをよく憶えています。母はよく、写生にも連れていってくれました。その時期に絵をたくさん描いていたことが、フラワーデザインの仕事にも影響していると思います。

花を通じて、誰かの人生や暮らしに彩りを添えることができる仕事を、神様が私に与えてくれたことに感謝しています。

最後に、出版にあたり全面的に協力してくれた第一園芸には、感謝してもしきれません。私の無理をいつも聞いていただき、すばらしい写真にしてくださった中島清一先生には本当に感謝しております。また、多くの作品を編集で仕上げてくださった山口未和子さんには大変お世話になりました。そして素敵に翻訳していただいた横田佳世子さんのほか、たくさんの方のおかげで、本書を出版することができました。岡 寛之さん、橋口 学さん、吉開千代さん、杉山絵里香さんには特に心より御礼申し上げます。

新井光史

Koji Arai 新井光史

Born in Kōbe, Japan, in 1960. Migrated to Brazil in order to work as a flower grower. An increasing interest in design and floral creations led to a job at a florist in Sao Paolo, where he discovered the possibilities of self-expression in the medium of 'flowers'. Following his return to Japan, he joined Daiichi Engei in 1988. After managing projects for major hotels where his responsibilities included designing wedding decorations and planning and developing new products, he currently heads the Daiichi Engei Design Team. His work ranges from demonstrations at events, conducting workshops, devising wedding and party decorations, to creating bespoke flower arrangements. His motto and plan is 'to etch a permanent memory of the ephemeral beauty of flowers that we long to linger over because it is so fleeting', while he continues to carve out his distinctive path in flower design.

Key achievements and awards

2000: Winner of the Flower Design Competition, International Orchid Festival
Winner of Objets Competition, Tokyo Cup
2008: First Prize and Prime Minister's Award, JFTD Japan Cup
2011: Japanese contestant at the Intercontinental Cup of Flower Design in Taiwan (5th place).
2016: Demonstration at Japan Grand Prix International Orchid Festival
Winner, Round Four of Hanaike Battle REAL
2017: Second place in Fusion Flower International Designer of the Year competition (organized by Fusion Flowers Magazine, UK)

Publications

Hana-Suppli: Shiawase Ippai Kotoba-no-Hanataba 120 (Floral Supplements for Joy: 120 Bouquets of Inspiring Quotes), Rai-cho Sha, 2012
Supervising Editor of Flower Arranging Ideas Book: Hana Ippon kara Daily ni Tanoshimu (Flower Arrangements Idea Book: Everyday Pleasures Starting From a Single Bloom), GAKKEN plus, 2017

1960年神戸生まれ。花の生産者としてブラジルへ移住、その後、サンパウロの花屋で働くことになり表現することに目覚める。帰国後、1988年 第一園芸に入社。ホテル店の店長としてウェディング装花や商品企画部門などを経て、現在は第一園芸デザイン室の室長を務める。イベントでのデモンストレーションやワークショップをはじめ、ウェディングやパーティ装飾、オーダーメイドアレンジメントのご提案など幅広く活動を行う。
「儚いからこそ、いつまでも心に残しておきたい花の一瞬の美しさを永遠の記憶として心に残す」ことをモットーに、独自のフラワーデザインを追求し続けている。

主な受賞歴

2000年 世界蘭展フラワーデザイン部門にて最優秀賞受賞
東京カップ オブジェ部門にて最優秀賞受賞
2008年 ジャパンカップ・フラワーデザイン競技会にて優勝、内閣総理大臣賞受賞
2011年 インターコンチネンタルカップ・フラワーデザイン競技会(台湾)に日本代表として参加、5位入賞
2014年 花いけバトルSPIN OFFシリーズ「IFEX 特別編」WINNER
2016年 世界らん展日本大賞2016にてデモンストレーション
花いけバトルREAL第四戦 WINNER
2017年 イギリス園芸誌「フュージョンフラワー」主催 Fusion Flower International Designer of the Year にて総合2位入賞

書籍

著書『花サプリ しあわせいっぱい、ことばの花束120』(雷鳥社/2012年)
監修『フラワーアレンジアイデアBOOK:花1本からデイリーに楽しむ』(学研プラス/2017年)

Author
Koji Arai 新井光史
k-arai@daiichi-engei.co.jp

Photography
Kiyokazu Nakajima 中島清一
kiyo10917@gmail.com

Text and Editing
Mikako Yamaguchi 山口未和子

English Translation
Kayoko Yokota 横田佳世子

Final Editing
Katrien Van Moerbeke

Lay-out
Group Van Damme
www.groupvandamme.eu

Supported by
Daiichi Engei Co., Ltd. 第一園芸株式会社
6th Toshin Building 8F 1-5-21 Katsushima, Shinagawa-ku Tokyo 140-0012, Japan
〒140-0012 東京都品川区勝島1-5-21 東神ビル6号館
Tel +81-3-6404-1300
Fax +81-3-6404-1302
http://www.daiichi-engei.jp/

Published by
Stichting Kunstboek bvba
Legeweg 165
8020 Oostkamp
Belgium
Tel +32 50 46 19 10
Fax +32 50 46 19 18

ISBN 978-90-5856-584-6
D/2017/6407/18
NUR 421

Printed in the EU